POEMS
FROM THE
Heart

BY BRENT JONES

Christian Living Books, Inc.
Largo, MD

ISBN 978-1-56229-025-2

Christian Living Books, Inc.
P. O. Box 7584
Largo, MD 20792
ChristianLivingBooks.com

Unless otherwise indicated, Scripture quotations are taken from the King James Version of the Bible.

Printed in the United States of America

DEDICATION

I would like to dedicate this book to all the people who supported and believed in me. To my wife, Tracy, Brent Jr., Davon, Clori, Brannon and my Pastor, YaQuis Shelley. Thank you for having the faith to believe in me. God Bless!

CONTENTS

ACKNOWLEDGEMENTS

First and foremost, I would like to thank my Lord and Savior, Christ Jesus for loving me enough to die on the cross for me.

I would like to thank my father and mother for always being there when I needed you the most and encouraging me to have faith enough to write this book.

I would like to thank my sons, Brent Jr. and Davon, for being born and making my life worth living. You two have been the biggest blessings in my life. It has been an honor watching you grow into great men of God. I couldn't love anyone more.

To my niece, Sadé, who has always had a smile on her face… since birth. I have always been proud of you and Chynia for having that love in your heart for people.

To Clori and Brannon, thank you for always being there for me when I needed you and understanding me when I didn't even understand myself.

Lastly, to my wonderful wife, Tracy, thank you for supporting me in everything that I say and do. Thank you for loving me with the love of Christ. I love you with all my heart. You are my true angel.

BRENT & DAVON

There is so much stuff
that I want to say.
So let me get it out
and start this way.
Brent and Davon
I'm so proud of you
the way you have grown
and things you went through.
I know in the beginning
you didn't see my flaws.
Growing up as little kids
you didn't see them at all.
But as you got older,
as we all do,
you see your father wasn't perfect
trying my best to raise you.
I guess what I'm saying
is the mistakes that I made,
affected you a lot,
and in more than one way.
You both had a great childhood
and for that I feel blessed,
being raised by a family
that gave their very best.
You never got caught up

in sex, fighting or drugs.
All you seen, was never mean,
just a family full of love.
Raising you as a father
has been the greatest joy
in my life.
In the future,
I'll still be here
to continue to fight.
Fight for what?
You may ask.
To be your father and live.
For all the mistakes I made
I pray you can forgive.
I read in God's Word
that when we create sin
we have to pay in some way.
That's the world we live in.
But Jesus died for all
and that's what you know.
So forgive me without hate
and that's what you show.
Other people can't do it,
but you two are my boys,
who I will continue to love
with patience and poise.
So how do I tell you?
Where do I begin?
In a room full of people,
about my own sin...
I cheated on your step mom.
I'm really selfish at times.
I used to curse like a sailor.

But in that area I'm fine.
I lie from time to time.
God's working with me on that.
I don't make a lot of money
and my car runs like crap.
I can't afford a house
that you can call your own
and because of my sin,
I'm lonely and alone.
But thank God I'm alive
and things will change,
because everything I do,
Is now in Christ's name.
As long as I'm alive
I will take care of you,
wherever you go,
or what you go through.

Brent Jr, Brent Sr, Davon, Claymont, DE. 1999

I WOULD JUST BE

Without God I would be nothing
(But He gave me life)
Without my parents I would be nothing
(But they raised me with love)
Without my sister and brother I would be nothing
(But they made sure I was loved)
Without my best friend I would be nothing
(But it was someone I could talk to)
No doubt, without Jesus I would be nothing
(Because He died for me) WOW!
And at this very moment
I realize that without all these people
I would never have been the man
I am today
For that I'm grateful and say thank you
Because I never really opened my eyes to see
That without all of you...
I would just be.

VICTIM

Another one gone. You sit and say why.
To be a victim of the streets to let another one die.
Learn to take a fall when the crazy fall comes.
Without a gun you better run
because no matter where you come from,
From New York to L.A. Many people getting slayed.
Gunshots getting popped every day in every way.
It's the will to will and it's hard I know.
Even though ya making dough,
There is nowhere else to go.
Stuck in the projects trying to get out.
Cash flow in your pockets
So without a doubt you have clout.
At least you think that and then come the drive by.
Not paying attention cause the weed
has got you so high.
Five of your friends dead and you were the sixth.
A set up was prosperous so you got fixed.
But living in the ghetto doesn't mean you have to live down
Back in the streets and now you never come around.
Dealing with the crack heads standing on the corner,
They tell you "Take a hit" you say "NO".
But then, you gonna.
What a crazy way to live getting high for a friend.
When your friend really the devil,

But won't tell you til the end.
It's the same, year in and year out.
Around doing drugs, hanging out.
Not ever trying to see, think or know what life's about.
The ghetto's just a name. Where you live is what you make it.
Every day, in every way, you have to reach out and take it.
So let me say this, before I run out of time.
You'll pay the price if you do the crime.

WHEN WILL IT END

A little girl, I knew for many years
took care of herself.
No one else was there.
Daddy out in the streets, stealing for money.
Mama died, doing the rock, way far from funny.
She depended on strength and strength alone.
Slept where ever she could didn't have a home.
Got caught up early in the world of sex.
No leader in her life she's 10 and now pregnant.
Little money and not a bit of support.
Now the baby... she will have to abort.
I remember when she was just five.
I use to come over when her mama was still alive.
I told her Mama to stop doing the crack.
She just looked at her baby and told me to "GET BACK".
I would see the girl sit there and cry.
Now a junkie on the street at 10
And you wonder why.
A perfect life about to begin
Turned bad which is sad.
When Will It End?
A friend named Tim was a friend for life.
But with the things that he did, he wasn't living right.
I asked him to change and the time was now.
Tim said he would but claimed "I don't know how?"

Running from the cops every day on the hour.
Not knowing his life would so be devoured.
I tried to help him every day I could.
But he got caught up hanging in the wrong neighborhood.
He tried to bring me in, as I tried to bring him out.
Night after night I would hear him shout.
Scream at his mother throw hands with his father.
It didn't bother him, but me, it bothered.
So I left Tim alone, didn't follow his tracks.
But he kept on going and didn't look back.
So that was it. What else could I do?
"Nothing!" Tim said and that our friendship was through.
Four months passed and Tim never called me.
Hoping he was alright, so I went to see.
His mother was crying as she opened the door.
Tim was shot and killed, trying to rob a liquor store.
Well, that was that and now Tim is gone.
But to me, his spirit will still live on.
It's really bad, as I say again.
My friend's gone but still lives on. When will it end?

My Crazy Girlfriend

I threw a party at my crib one Saturday night.
Had all my boys there and the party was tight.
Then my girl came over and she started to trip.
Because a lot of guys over so I told her to dip.
She said, "I can't stay over?"
I said, "What do you think?"
"You have a problem with my boys and your attitude stinks!"
Then she said, "I'll stop tripping if you make them go home."
Then I said, like Michael Jackson, "Just leave me alone."
"Cause I don't have time to deal with your crap!"
She said, "Your boys are all here so you think you're all that!"
I took a big sigh then I said, "Okay."
Just like burger king, you can have it your way.
So, everybody left but the party was def.
Laid down to go to sleep and three hours I slept
Before my girl woke me up and said,
"Go to the store!"
I said, "I kicked my boys out and now you want more!"
That's when I kicked her out, no questions were asked.
I just threw clothes out with all of her bags.
Then, I gave her some money. She said, "What's this for?"
I said, "Take a darn cab!"
Then, I slammed the door.

Uncle Cliff

A lot of things I'm thinking, in the back of my mind
When I got a phone call from a pal of mine.
He sounded kind of sad; I knew something was wrong.
He sounded pretty weak, but what he said was strong.
Concerning Uncle Cliff and what he did,
To his own wife, not to mention his kid.
He shot them both and to this day,
Really don't know why, but let's keep it that way.
Uncle Cliff was a good man, no doubt about that.
When Tim and I would come over, he would sit and chat with us.
Good conversations that we all adored.
And what we had in common was serving the Lord.
Uncle Cliff was loving, caring, and nice.
But I guess things like this happen in life.
I just wished it didn't happen to my Uncle Cliff.
But, I still love him and the things he left
Were really good even though he was wrong.
The positive things still linger along in my mind.
And I think it's time, to stay and start to pray.
While writing this rhyme,
I'll remember him as a hero and a preacher.
He taught us a lot so he was a good teacher.
But it's sad, once again, and such a shame
That the life he was leading went down the drain.

My Love For You

My love for you transcends all time and space.
And in my heart you hold a very special place.
With you, I don't know I could live.
Because my undying love for you I could no longer give.
My heart hurts so much when I'm away from you.
Only the sound of your voice on the phone gets me through
Until the time that I see you once more,
We have so much fun together and I never know what's in store.
The hugs, the kisses, the soft loving words you say
Let me know that being with you is the only way
To find true happiness and the "til death do us part" kind of love,
The kind of love that can only come from our heavenly Father,
from above.
I've given you the key to my very heart
And don't want to be without you, and without apart.

A Letter To My Lord

Lord, sometimes I don't understand the things that You do.
But even when I don't, I still love You,
Because You gave me life when it was no need to be given,
Cause you kept me strong to go on to keep living.
And no matter where I go in this world You're there,
To hold my hand, To share... To care...
Your love is greater than any sunset.
You're an awesome God than any father can get.
My mom and dad, I love them so much.
It's because You touched them for me to be touched,
Your inner mystery is powerful indeed,
To know what people want and the things we all need.
You let things happen for a reason, of course.
So we can really see who is the boss.
Well, thank You, Lord, for Your love and time.
And for making me yours as I made You mine.

I Just Can't Stop

I can't stop thinking about you,
No matter how hard I try.
I can't stop thinking about you,
and I wonder why?
MAN! I haven't felt this way
in a long period of time.
Should I stop thinking this way?
Dreaming you may be mine?
That's crazy I guess,
Being we just met.
I'm just ready to be settled,
And in my ways I am set.
You are too, as I know for a fact.
Got a great job, so there's nothing you lack.
We like the same things.
To me, that's a plus.
Both like to talk without being stuck up.
Maybe, it's too soon to give this gift to you.
After what you told me,
And what you been through.
But, I'm taking my chance,
While I am on top.
But thinking about you,
I just can't stop.

Why Ask Why

Why ask why about things you know
When you should go on and let life flow.
Why ask why when you're gonna get in trouble.
Just take the punishment like a man and on the double.
Why ask why about stuff when it's there staring you in the face
and you still say where?
Why ask why about old things.
Do you see how much trouble a question can bring?
So just leave it alone and you still ask why.
A fanatic you attack I say stop you say "I'll try"
A useless saying that you have to say
"So go on and say it" you say "NO" I say "You may"
You might as well say it cause eventually you will.
It will come back around like a windmill.
It's just a common word of everyday life
Like getting shot with a gun or stabbed with a knife.
That's just something that usually happens.
Ask why if you want but I'm done rapping!

Dreams Held Back

When you hold your dreams back
People want to know.
When people can care less
you want to let go.
Is it wrong for me
to keep my dreams inside?
Or am I just confused
with thoughts I try to hide.
Most people can see though
what a person is going through.
The feeling I feel
is a state of mind
That is hard to understand
even for me sometimes.
But as long as the dreams
I have exist,
The passion for thought
will never be missed!

SUPERMAN

I was lying in my bed 12:00 at night.
Superman picked me up and we flew out of sight.
We took off like a rocket on the fourth of July.
Then, I realized it's a dream 'cause I can't fly.
But, I went along with it since that was the plan.
Me flying in the air with Superman.
We stopped in New York for a bite to eat.
Then, we helped an old lady go across the street.
We had a good time cause the city was the place.
Superman got bored; so, we flew into space.
Man, it was incredible; so, I had to see more.
Superman said, "Okay." Then, he gave me a tour.
He said, "Here's the Big Dipper."
Then, we jetted to Mars.
On the way down, I hit a couple of stars.
What a sight to see; there were people like me.
But they talked and acted real strange and crazy.
Then, we took off to Saturn, Venus and Pluto.
We stayed to see the Martian put on a show.
I couldn't believe it. We flew around the world.
Then, Superman showed off and gave the globe a twirl.
I told him to chill and let's go back to earth.
He said, "After you." So, I went first.
We flew around for an hour; then, I checked my watch.
Time went by fast; it was 6 o'clock.

I had to go but O thanked him much.
He said, "I'll be around; so, keep in touch."
I had just enough energy to make it back home.
I crawled in the bed; then, I was alone.
I thought about the great fun I had.
A simple smile was on my face because space was bad!
I got up out the bed with a cape in my hand
Thinking, "What a great dream about Superman!"

Davon, Brent Sr, and Brent Jr, Bowie, MD. 2013

My Fear

I'm afraid of my fear
and my fear knows I'm scared.
No where to turn, no where to hide
And all this fear I have to bottle up inside.
To be strong for my kids.
Daddy why you cry?
Do I sit and lie?
I have something in my eye.
Inside my body I tremble, a nervous wreck.
My fear has me jumping
Do I know why?
Of course I do, know the fear inside.
Do you want to admit it? Yes I do.
But don't want to talk about it, so to who?
Give it to God.
He is the only one who understands it all.
From this one son.
This feeling surrounds me
Not letting me go.
Making sure it stays there
Just letting me know...
MY FEAR

It's The Little Things That Matter

It's the little things that matter.
Certain people don't realize
Just the simple things in life
A lot of us despise.
Like taking a walk with family and friends.
Instead of buying a car, like a Porsche or a Benz.
Being able to breathe or being able to run
or enjoy yourself playing when you're having fun.
Being able to talk and able to sing.
That's what I mean by all the little things.

Be thankful for what you have
because what you have is all you got.
You have to work for what you don't have
To get it all in one shot.
Knowing who you are, and feeling good about yourself
is the best thing in the world
to getting money or wealth
so... remember the little things.

Brent Jr, Sadé Jones, Davon, Bowie, MD. 2013

The Inner Mystery In Me

My mind goes blank sometimes when I think
about the inner mystery in me.
My mind goes sour and I drain all my power,
when I think of the inner mystery in me.
God hears our prayers, yet mine go astray.
Is there a reason? Lord why today?
Be wise, my child, someone once said to me,
To pick and choose, to win not lose.
So, I open and choose to see.
Then that someone disappeared
not taking its own advice.
Just vanished in the dark,
In the deepest of night.
I sit in my quiet room
wondering who I am.
Thinking I'm somebody important,
and other times not giving a damn.
Where there's a right, there's a wrong.
Where there's a weak, there's a strong.
You work hard to build yourself up.
Someone works even harder to break you down.
God came to this earth for one main reason,
To love us, so one day we could love Him.
I believe that's the inner mystery in me,
To love people like Christ loves us

But never having a discussion
with anyone to discuss.
I keep asking myself what am I worth.
To be conceived by a mother,
and dropped on this earth.
I understand how to work things.
I understand how to obey.
I understand how to listen
to the things that people say.
I understand how to drive.
I understand how to be a dad,
because I have the greatest one
in the world.
The greatest ever had.
I understand you have to work.
I understand you have to cook.
I understand if you want to be smart,
you have to pick up a book.
If something is dirty you clean it.
If you sin a lot then repent.
A lot of people don't know it.
But to me it's just common sense.
I understand when you're mad,
you will eventually calm down.
I understand when you search you'll see.
But what I don't understand,
God's number one plan,
The inner mystery I have in me.

My Boys

No matter how down I get
or feel my life's destroyed,
I can always look up
and be proud with a smile,
Because I have my boys.
There's nobody better
than Brent and Davon
that's why I am still here
That's why I go on.
I will always be there and never leave
And if I could, all the hurt I would retrieve
From the things they will go through
In pain of everyday life.
But all I can do, is be there for you two
To teach you right from wrong.
Ever since you both got here, you have always been close.
The way you love each other is what I cherish the most.
Daddy will always love you
No matter where I'm at
My Boys

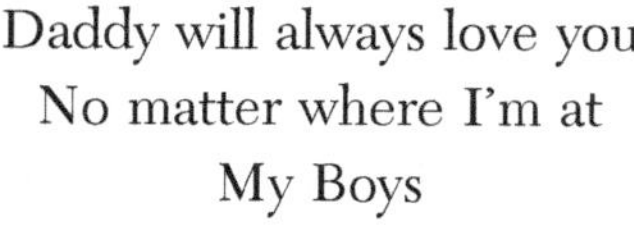

**Brent Jr, Brent Sr, and Davon
at home, Mitchellville, MD. 2001**

Losing Someone

When you lose someone it hurts for a time.
There's nothing you can do,
but go on with life.
When you keep on losing,
and there's nowhere to turn,
usually they turn on their own self,
Because they figure why should I go on?
Sometimes people should stop
and think, "Is this what I really want?"
Most of the time, it isn't,
but don't know how to end the problem,
so they go on until the problem ends them.

The Rodney King Case

"I Saw The Tape"

I saw the tape. Of course, you heard about it.
Not guilty wasn't right. There's no doubt about it.
A black man on the ground being beaten doesn't matter,
By four white cops, now his dreams could be shattered.
In the court room is where they got away clean.
So where does that leave us and all this mean?
It means that anytime they want to,
They can arrest, prosecute, or even beat you.
The thing that bothers and really gets me
Is they had the tape for everyone to see.
Was it because they were white and he was black?
To throw him out the car and beat him like that?
Overall, it's not right for them to get away.
That's a fact but opinion cause the jury has the say.
It would be hard to go on forgiving,
knowing that the cops are beating and killing.
But what's so shocking and really messed up,
Is they had the proof and it was still not enough.
Well, I'll tell you one thing about this case,
I know the truth cause I saw the tape.

The tape showed it all about what they did.
Now, how do you go back and tell your kid
What happened to him will never happen to you.

by Brent Jones

That lie you abide by to cover the truth
How many people will they have to drop
In the police force just to make the law stop?
Rodney King was almost beat to death
On the ground, bruised up, and out of breath.
In the city of L.A. is where it started.
Riots broke out and people broken hearted
Burning up everything left and right
Not caring about the law cause the law isn't right.
In this situation there was no hesitation.
People burning everything down in frustration.
It's a black and white issue in a big way
About the Rodney King case that we see today
People in L.A. are on a mission
To see about the right case but the wrong decision.
And if you say they're not guilty get out of my face
Because the proof is there cause I saw the tape.

A Place In This World

A place in this world can it really be?
A place in this world that fits only me.
Sometimes I think that this world
was meant for someone other than me.
Like God made a mistake,
but that could never be.
I daydream a lot and look into the sky
and feel like I'm standing still,
as the rest of the world zooms by.
A lonely place on this earth,
is the dark feeling I hate,
not knowing who's out there,
I can call soul mate.
Will that day ever come when I say to myself
that my eyes start to run,
to seek the right person to help.
I keep asking myself, "When will I get married?"
I keep asking myself, "Who is my friend?"
I keep asking myself, "What burdens will I carry?"
and "Where is the girl that God will send?"
These answers I have no idea of.
These answers I wish I knew.
It would give me comfort and peace
through my soul and spirit too.

by Brent Jones

Knock, Knock. Who's there?
I would open up and say
A place in this world
Can you come out and play?
I would jump at the chance
To find my place, to be comfortable in life.
I would stay there and be safe.
But every morning I wake up
The world is like a dream,
A maze without direction,
A note without the letters,
Letters without words.
So the words were never made out clearly
Enough to ever be heard.
These are only my feelings
And the emotions on where I should be.
Not really to know, what direction to go
So I keep praying and wait to see.
The rain that falls at night, makes the whole entire world cease.
That's when I find my place in this world
Because the whole world, like me,
Is at peace.

My Own Way

I remember when I was little
My mother us to say,
No matter what the crowd is doing,
Always go your own way.
I always wondered why. I never really knew
Until I got older to see what people do
Smoking, stealing, robbing, killing,
Nobody does these things alone.
They try to make others join in
And if you don't, they call you chicken.
What God created as sin,
like Jesus turn the other cheek.
That's what I usually do.
If something's wrong, that's going on,
I see and flee from the crew.
Innocent people are in jail now,
By going the same way and didn't know how.
To say how they really felt,
So they went along.
Now got life behind bars,
And now their life is gone.
So if the crowd says, "Let's do this!"
I just simply say, "No thanks, everybody"
and go my own way.

A Broken Heart

I have a broken heart. Yes, indeed, I do.
I try to be strong for myself,
from the things that I'm going through.
I seen what I saw then I couldn't believe,
That you told me to leave and ask for the key.
That crushed me all over and then instead,
I was the one on the couch,
while he was the one in the bed,
and the crazy thing is...
well maybe not crazy to you…
but you knew it hurt me,
and said screw it, we're through.
All the time away from me, how can I cry?
The only thing I can do now is ask myself, "Why?"
I just wish I didn't see your new lover and friend
and knowing your relationship with him,
is just about to begin.
Well, after seven years, I lost out.
Then again, lost in love with you,
to be reduced to just "a friend."
Because we have kids together,
two handsome young men,
which doesn't make it any better.
So, all I can do is wish the best for you,
while my broken heart will stay,

until time takes it away. What else do I say?
MAN, it's hard, every day.
I think about what I saw and knowing you want more,
with someone other than me is killing me.
Right now, I'm jealous and down.
I look around, and no one's around,
just me looking and feeling stupid.
It's easy to capture someone's heart to fill it up.
But, a broken heart like mine only needs time,
to mend, over a used to be lover,
and a very good friend.

RACISM

Racism is a word that can go both ways.
No matter what it is as long as one gets paid.
Who really cares about a black insane
or a black who shot a white with a bullet to the brain.
The only ones cared was the ones that knew him.
The ones that didn't care are the ones that would do him.
It has to be more than just a race or color,
Because blacks on blacks are killing one another,
Not thinking at all that's why they call us animals,
Killing each other like Hannibal the cannibal.
Racism, to me, goes far beyond that.
No matter what color, whether black or white.
Because the person you are, which inside you,
Is what makes you react and do the things that you do.
You have to learn who you are before you judge other people.
Because no matter what color you are we are all equal.
But you say, "OK, I can live whit this"
with the world like it is, yea that's a dis.
That you made to yourself and try to cover it up
but if one steps wrong then you will erupt.
Learn to stay strong like Rosa Parks or Shirley Chisholm,
and cut the madness and stop the racism.
Racism I can't stand but who's to really blame?
The slave or slave owners who gave us different names?
Back then it was cool to hate one another

Cause the whites controlled the blacks every day
because of color.
Black people were mad and had the right to be.
Cause you're hit with a whip. Of course it makes you crazy.
Living a life without a life to live.
So you're better off dead because your soul you give
To the man in the white who gets to rape your wife,
While you sit in strife and want to kill him with a knife.
But instead you cry because there's nothing you can do.
So you sit and morn until the feeling passes through,
Which is really never does so you try to cope,
that one day around the corner there will be hope.
You can't take it no more as you start to run,
from the gun pointed at being targeted as the one.
Feeling bad already also dead and insane
While to the men in the white this is nothing but a game.
One shot goes thru you, two more quickly follow,
as you fall to the ground your mind becomes hollow.
Your brain starts to swell and as it gets bigger,
The last words before you die that you heard was
"DUMB NIGGER."
That's deep! You have to admit it.
And racism… Quit it!

Still Working With Me

Through all the bad things I've done,
You're still working with me.
Through the bad things I've seen,
You're still working with me.
It's hard to believe that You love me that much.
Don't You know what I've done?
And You still consider me Your number one?
Your love is such a mystery.
I will never understand.
But I know You loved me
When You turned me into a man.
To come to this earth
And die a brutal death.
To take 39 slashes and a spear to the chest.
Knowing the outcome of all of that
To You, Lord Jesus, I take off my hat.
Your mercy is incredible.
Your peace no one can deny.
Every time we are in trouble
You hear every cry.
What a great world that we live in
Where You control us and forgive our sins.
You love me, that much, so now I see
No matter what's done
You're working with me.

A Passionate Kiss

There is something about a passionate kiss
That's makes my world just spin
In a passionate place
On a passionate date
Like under the stars
Kissing in the wind
The kiss is so gentle and soft
It puts your body in a zone
Up in the sky
On a natural high
Just you and that person alone
Feelings have a lot to do with the kiss
And knowing your feelings are true
So wherever you go your love will show
In what you say
As well as what you do
So "Kiss me you fool" she would say
And as our lips begin to touch
She looks deep in me
In my eyes to see
As she says "I love you so much"
Now that's my definition of
A PASSIONATE KISS!

Dreams In A Glass Jar

I put a glass jar by my bed so when I sleep,
I can save all the dreams that I really want to keep.
There are some really great dreams that I have sometimes.
I transform the memories to the jar from my mind.
Even some of the bad dreams, I sometimes keep too.
To remind me where I've been and what I've been through.
I don't have to be awake to lay and elate,
As long as I am dreaming and in a dream state.
The fantasy comes and goes like the wind,
That's why I have the jar to put my fantasy in.
I dream all of the time so the jar gets full,
So I pile them in files and from the files I pull
When the sky goes black and the rain come down,
And I'm left all alone when no one else is around.
The peace I feel I could never express,
That's when good things come when I'm at my best.
There are some dreams that I quickly go through.
Then some dreams I have over like déjà vu.
The nightmares I have I really don't like,
But I learn from those dreams,
which makes everything alright.
But no matter what
I dream about
Whether near or far
I will always store my dreams
in my big glass jar.

A Leaf Falls

A leaf falls from above
Without making a sound
Hitting branch after branch
On its way to the ground
As the weather changes season
The leaf changes color
Not knowing where the wind will take it
From one day to another
The invisible wind
that's so fresh and free
makes itself known
blowing with its dignity
turning calm waters to ripples
In each day of the week
as that leaf goes and blows
with the wind at its feet
Now here comes the rain
hitting hard to the ground
On top of that leaf
which makes the leaf brown
A half an hour later the sun comes out
shining on the world
as the world moves about
Making everything hot
blazing 90 degrees

by Brent Jones 

Disintegrating the leaf
Breaking piece after piece
The wind blows again
seeming cruel at this time
blowing pieces of the leaf
in different directions the pieces fly
A new season moves in
where the flowers bloom
And the kids get out of school
in the month of June
Nature is happy once more
people and all
Until three months later
you see a leaf fall.

LITTLE CHILD

Hey little child come walk with me
in a land far away
that only we can see
Hey little child come feel the cool breeze
in a magical land
that listens to your needs
Hey little child don't be alarmed
I'm here to protect you
from every kind of harm
Hey little child can you see the sun
Where we're standing it's cold
so over to it lets run
Faster and faster and faster we sore
You slip then you trip
I pick you up once more
Making sure we're together
cause I care that much
Holding your little hand
so that we both can be touched
Going at life's problems
first me and then you
Being there through it all and
as you go through
Knowing how important
you are to me

by Brent Jones

Hey little child
can you see what I see?
Little child you're the door
that has opened my life
and I walk through that door
without any strife
Hey little child here I am
with open arms and open hands
Ready to hug you
Ready to care
Ready to love you
Waiting to share
To share all the love that is in me
with you alone so that you can see
what I feel for you is deep in my heart
Don't want to be without you and without you apart
Hey little child don't look so sad
For all this time I've been your dad
So I will be with you forever
Not just a little while
For you will be
always to me
My special Little Child.

Brent Sr and Brent Jr at Kingsford Elementary School, Mitchellville, MD. 2004

DEEP LOVE

Love came from deep down inside
And most of the time love is something that you can't hide
The emotion is expressed in so many ways
Between the things you do and the things you say
That's why this poem means so much to me
To give to you with open eyes to see
I say thanks to the creator that is up above
For giving me a person like you to love
Not just as a lover but also a friend
Who understands my needs from beginning to end
That's why I say thanks God for bringing me you
To understand love the way that I do

King Of Hearts

You don't have to be black or white to be loved
You don't have to have a purse to get mugged
You don't have to sing or dance to be good
You don't have to wait too late to say I should
have done what I did when I had the chance to do it

Just try to abide to make it and pursue it
You don't have to be rich just to be on top
You don't have to be cool when you know you're not
Cause people should like you for who you are
and if they don't then forget them by far
Don't get hurt cause you thought you had a friend
if he wasn't there before then he won't be there in the end

Just keep on moving until you find another
Who won't hurt you but be there as a brother
Someone you know without a doubt
and that's what the King of Hearts is all about
The King of Hearts

What the King of Hearts is
is someone with a big heart
to do anything whether dumb or smart
to be accepted in a group to fit in
To do anything for a friend
And once the friend knows that his heart is big

He'll try to take advantage and the deeper he'll dig

With emotions and feelings that you might have
While they think it's a joke to sit back and laugh
It can happen to a boy or even a girl
You, me or anybody who is in the world
Because the heart is there and we all have to use it
But in the right way don't let one abuse it

The only one you should give your heart to
Is God and Jesus cause They understand you
that's a real fact They will give you a hand
As the King of Hearts is the name of this jam.
The King of Hearts

Have you ever heard the saying "you don't have a heart"
Well, that's not true it's always been there from the start
It's just when you get real mad at someone
you take it out on them and that's not fun
When you're on your own then you can't be king

To be what you want and do everything
But when you're trapped inside with a doubt in mind
it doesn't make it any better so relax and unwind
Make it easy on yourself and let your heart rest
But be alert while you're in the progress
Never let anyone steal your dream
Because you know everything is not always how it seems

So get a grip on yourself and understand
Whether you're a boy, girl, lady, man or even a friend
Treat people the way you want to be treated
That's another saying but that saying is not needed
Unless you feel down and out or not wanted

by Brent Jones

Don't wait to get help just get right on it
This makes a difference right from the start
So be the best you can be with
The King of Hearts

WHERE DO WE STAND

I don't want to say it but it's true
about all of the killing and the drugs we do
You hear it on the radio everyday
and on the news "stop the violence" that's what they say

The saying's so common many people just ignore it
Like they never even heard it or maybe never saw it
There's different opinions from Whites and Blacks
Like 4 pens and a pencil and the pencil doesn't match

If you're hearing what I'm saying then listen to me clearly
Stop the violence to me is just another theory
Because crime is crime and it's not gonna stop
No matter where you look another brother's getting dropped

Like a help wanted sign when you need help
But until the time comes you're by yourself
It's just an example of what I'm saying
so don't take it light cause on the streets we're slaying
other people for their money, cars, or just to do it
Then you end up in jail for a crime so you blew it

REACH ONE TO TEACH ONE

We have to fight united and do what is right
So we might not lose the sight of our life
That God has given us with tremendous power
Do you know a black brother gets killed every hour

And the reason why over a reputation
It's sad but it happens in this nation
Stay strong to belong in the world supply
Because living on the edge means "do or die"
Being on crack or shooting up with a needle
The government makes it seem right when it's illegal

Mother crying, black brother dying
On the foul streets and nobody trying
to give a brother or a sister any dap
Instead they like to see the black race get slapped
There has to be a way that the brother understands
We have to reach and teach is the number one plan

Davon and Brent Sr, Mitchellville, MD. 2002

How Could You Hurt The One You Love

I hurt the one I loved. I meant to do it.
I just wish I could turn back the clock
and been faithful and honest.
Now there's no second chance for me.
My eyes are open and now I see,
that no matter what, you have to be true
in a relationship.
I usually am. It's just the sex that got in the way.
Losing my girl is the price I pay.
We hurt God all the time yet we say we love Him.
Is it the same with human life?
God forgives us time after time.
People sometimes do too,
but they never forget what you do.
Like me sometimes, you don't get second chances.
So make every day count with whoever you're with,
because you never know how much you will suffer
without that person in your life.
Once they're gone...they're gone.
So remember from my experience.
Be true...
Be you...
and never hurt the one you love.

Until The Next Day

I came home from work one afternoon.
The phone rang twice. It was my wife, I assumed.
I ran to the phone to check the caller ID.
I didn't recognize the number, so it wasn't for me.
So I got some lunch cause I was feeling kind of low.
Then I went to Billy Blanks to do some Tae Bo.
After I was done, I went to take a shower.
When I was finished, I got out.
I checked the clock to see the hour.
I went back downstairs to turn off the ringer.
Cut on the TV to watch some Jerry Springer,
then laid down to sleep and slept the night away,
and didn't wake up until the next day.

I woke up the next morning,
with my boys to play ball.
Then the girls wanted to go shopping,
so I took them to the mall.
The boys went too to get some gear to wear,
while the girls stayed in the salon,
getting styles done to their hair.
Then we all piled up and got in the van.
Took off to the beach to play in the sand.
So we got to the beach. The kids played in the water.
Then we all got hungry so Chinese food we all ordered.

We all ate a lot then laid down on the beach.
Got real relaxed then fell straight asleep.
The weather was nice. We slept the night away
and didn't wake up until the next day.

Dont Stray Away

Sweetheart, please, I need you in my life.
Without you, girl, there is stress and strife (that I feel).
The pain is so devastating,
Plus the fact that we're not talking is the part that I'm hating.
There has to be a way I can explain to you.
Instead of walking out after all we been through.
This girl is just a friend. So, please understand.
You're the only one for me. I am a really good man.
I will never keep secrets hid up in my mind.
But I'll let you know everything, line by line.
As they will come up, you will know.
And, all my love for you will show.
So, please don't go or even say no.
This friend that I have,
could never take your place.
I would be with her if that's the case.
We've been together six years, just to be exact.
So don't think I would cheat right behind your back.
Just listen to me and things will be okay.
I'm asking you, girl. Don't stray away.

When you curse, you know it hurts me,
but you don't even care.
My tolerance level is high and harder to bear.
The thought of losing you to an unworthy cause,

makes me think, "Do you love me or did you at all?"
To stray away keeps you from me and that I can't take.
So, before you decide, just hold up and wait.
Think about my feelings and the reason for this purpose.
Do you think I'd even try if I really did deserve this?
A friend is a friend but you're my girl and lover.
I don't two time so there is no other.
So, think about it sweetie, cause I love you so much.
We are meant to be. We're not put together by luck.
Together, we'll go through it, day by day.
So, I say once again. Don't stray away.

WHY DO I CRY?

Why do I cry when you're not coming back?
Why do I cry when there things I lack?
Why do I feel the way that I feel?
Maybe because this feeling is real.
Why do I cry when I know you don't want me?
A lack of disbelief hits my eyes so I can't see.
I guess I'm just blind to the fact,
that someone else is holding you,
and making love to you the way I used to.
The thought is killing me!
Why does it have to be him?
Why can't it be me?
The pain, the hurt, the jealously you caused,
Do you still love me?
Or did you ever at all?
God, I wish this feeling would just go away,
but it stays and plays,
with me every single day.
I used to daydream a lot and now in the same place,
that I was at 13, daydreaming in space,
about you and him and how happy you are.
Doing things for him like letting him drive your car.
You never let me do that.
There was always an excuse,
that went along with the yelling and mental abuse.

So, why do I cry?
Maybe it was because I loved you
and one day, long ago, you loved me too.

HOW SPECIAL YOU ARE

I'm so lucky to have you in my life,
through the good, bad, tough times and strife.
But in this relationship, I realize one thing,
how special you are, with the love you bring.
When we're not together, I do feel lonely,
because you're the one, my one and only.
Through summer, spring, whatever the season,
God put us together for a special reason.
So, as the grass is green, and the sky is blue,
you need to know that I love you.

One Day at a Time

Even though I feel I'm losing my mind,
God sustains me one day at a time.
All the mistakes I made to the lies I told,
were mistakes that I made,
and they tend to get old.
I've been walking on thin ice,
and somehow fell right through.
Now, my lies come back to haunt me,
and stick to me like glue.
I lost the things I had,
because I didn't use my brain.
Now, in one quick turn,
Brent Jones got burned,
and now things are not the same.
But as long as I learn,
from the mistakes that I made,
and start doing all the right things,
I will be blessed and also refreshed,
in all and everything.
Now, all I can do is sit and find
that I have to take life,
one day at a time.

WILL NEVER CHANGE

One day, it was two years long.
Don't know how everything really went wrong.
We tried to work it out but we just couldn't.
Begged and pleaded to take us back but just wouldn't.
I tried very hard for both of us to stay together.
It wasn't now, so let it be now cause now it's never.
But everything that your mother and I been through,
the good that came out of all of this was you.
Now nothing else matters to me but you, son.
Since you were born, you been nothing but number one,
In my life, and that's how you'll forever stay,
until I'm dead and gone and God takes me away.
Now my life has a big empty side,
with feelings and emotions that I can't even hide.
But with you, Brent, I can surely go on,
by seeing your face every day I stay strong.
All of this seems just like a dream.
In a fantasy world that I'm kind of stuck between.
But realizing that reality is here,
I have to stand up, like a man, to face my fear.
To be that man, to take control,
To raise my son – so young – until he's old.
No matter what happens in life, I'll always feel the same,
because my love for you, Brent, will never change.

Certain things only happen for a reason,
but we try to deny because it's so hard believing
that something so good that you had is now gone.
Just walked away with memories that linger on.
Every day, I try to think of something new.
To occupy my mind and keep my mind off you.
Now, the past, I have to ignore,
and look ahead to all the things in store.
Every day, I ask God the reason why.
Haven't got an answer, yet, so I just cry.
Does this make sense, everything I'm going through?
Really don't know but wish that I knew.
All I know is that I love my son so
and would keep him, cherish him, and never let him go.
My friend, Tim, he also felt the same.
He took his baby from the mother when the baby came.
It's really messed up but then again it's true.
The way a woman leaves her child like she do.
But, Davon, you're in my life right now
and I will never leave you, no way and no how.
I thank God for a son like you
and everything that we been through.
No matter how you feel,
I will always feel the same,
because my love for you will never change.

My Father... My Hero

What you should know about my father is this: he is, first of all, a wonderful and great human being. If you had to go to war, you would want a guy like my father by your side.

As a kid, I never realized how much my father meant to me. He was a really quiet man that was always working hard – a behind the scenes kind-of-guy. He's someone who would never get in anyone's business unless he had to or was forced to. Trust me, you wouldn't want to make my father mad. He could slap you across a room before you realized you were hit! He is just that fast. What I love about my father is that he is the most humble man you will ever meet. Whether he has five dollars or five million dollars in the bank, he is still and forever more will be the same person.

Now, of course, I'm not saying he's perfect. No man is. But, with all my father's mistakes – that I know about – and all the mistakes that I don't, he has always been perfect to me.

If there was a man on earth that was close to being like Christ, my father would be at the top of the list. People that meet him for the first time ask him, "Are you a preacher?" That's the kind of love he shows without saying anything about the bible. The love of God is all in him.

There are two great things I admire and respect about my father. The first thing is that he loves God with everything in him. No matter where he goes, what he's done, who he's with, the Holy Spirit travels with him. I have studied this carefully. Being like my father, now, I see this more clearly than I did when I was a kid. When you're a kid, you pretty much take for granted the hard work your parents put in to raise you. If you live long enough and have a father like I have, you will one day appreciate it.

The second thing is – and to me the greatest thing ever – my father was there. It may sound so simple to other people. To me, it meant everything. He was always there for me, my sister and my brother. Even when he wasn't there, he was there. When he had to travel a lot with his job, for weeks at a time, we knew he would be coming back home again. When he came back home, he would bring us some kind of present back. Most of the time, it would be those plastic wings from Delta airlines!

There are a million other things I remember about my father. That's why, to me, that's the greatest thing. He gave us those memories and loved us throughout them all! I know, for a fact, my father loves me with all his heart. When things in school didn't go well, you were right there. You never left our mother, our mother never left you, even though you two had tough times, you stuck it out with each other.

My mother knew, in her heart, what kind of value my father had in him and what kind of man my dad really was despite the mistakes he made – and some of them were pretty bad. That takes a lot of love and a whole bunch of wisdom on my mother's part.

My mother knew just because someone makes a few mistakes that doesn't mean that's who they are. It's just an act that they carry out. And, that can be fixed. It's when the person keeps doing the same things, over and over again, and doesn't care, one way or the other, how the other person feels. That's when you realize that's just who this person is. I commend my mother for hanging in there because everybody makes mistakes. It's how you come back from those mistakes that make you a better person. And, my father is a great person. To me, dad, you never got the credit you deserve. Well, here it is, from your oldest son. I would die for you, ten times over, because

I love you that much. You're my father... My Hero!!

A True Love Story

A woman named Donna was born with AIDS. She told every man she met that she had the disease. No man wanted to be bothered with her until one day... Donna met this guy named Jay. Jay and Donna hit it off right, from the start. Then, after the first date, she told Jay she had AIDS. Jay told Donna that he loved her honesty and that he wanted to stay with her. Donna was so shocked. She thought he would run away like everyone else, but he didn't. After a year and a half of dating, Jay asked Donna to marry him. Donna couldn't believe it. She started crying and said "Yes!"

They got married and Jay took care of Donna and loved her every day of his life. Two years after they got married, Jay got sick. He contracted AIDS from Donna. But, it didn't matter, one bit. He told Donna that he loved her enough to suffer along with her, no matter what happens. That's how much he loved her. Three months later, Jay died. Donna was heartbroken. She thought about taking her life, early, but God got her through each day.

Eight months later, scientists found a cure for AIDS. Donna's life was saved. She was happy but then, again, heartbroken they hadn't found a cure before Jay passed away. Donna is now living in Dallas, Texas with her husband, David, and three kids. Even though Donna's moved on with her life, she will always remember the man that gave his life and loved her more than life itself. She will never forget her true love, Jay.

Sometimes I wonder, is love – or shall I say "true love" – worth dying for? What do you think?

When It Rains

When it rains, every thought of you is more intense
Because your love pours down on me,
like an intense rain shower every time I'm with you.
Old relationships we had are gone and we learned from them
to be stronger for each other as we move on,
move on to another chapter in life,
to that only rain cloud in the sky that makes life worth living,
to make every moment count as we fall from the sky,
lost in each other's love knowing only one thing,
that with God's love, through us,
we can and will survive all the rain storms
Satan tries to throw our way.
You know, it's easy to love someone on a sunny, beautiful day,
but harder on a gloomy rainy day.
I prefer those cold, wet days because that's when I sacrifice
myself into your world, into your zone, knowing I'm yours
and yours alone. As I stand in the middle of your world,
our world, that God made, the cold wet rain
hits my face like popcorn. I stand there with you,
holding your hand knowing how beautiful you are,
and freezing this moment in time.
For it is this moment that I capture and remember...
when it rains.

A Crazy Dream

I woke up at four in the morning and started to cry
because I was thinking real hard about you and I.
About how much I love you and to me how much you mean
That's when I laid down and started to dream.
I dreamed of a place in a far off land,
that you were my wife and I was holding your hand,
running in a big field as fast as we could,
and fell off a mountain into some dark scary woods.
We looked at each other as we were out of breath,
and nothing could prepare us for what came next.
A man rose up from right out of the ground.
Didn't know he was behind us cause he didn't make a sound.
We turned around quick then started backing up.
Then, without saying a word, he started walking toward us.
He was dressed like a bum and he smelled really bad.
He took the hat from his eyes and it was my dad!
He didn't look the same with that dirty old coat.
He fell to the ground and that's when he spoke.
Satan is here. He's watching you now.
You have to wake up, and I'll show you how,
to get out of these woods. Follow this stream;
It will lead you both straight out of this dream!
I said, "dad come with us." But his eyes turned red,
"This is not easy to say, but I'm already dead!"
That when a big bolt of lightning hit my father in the chest,

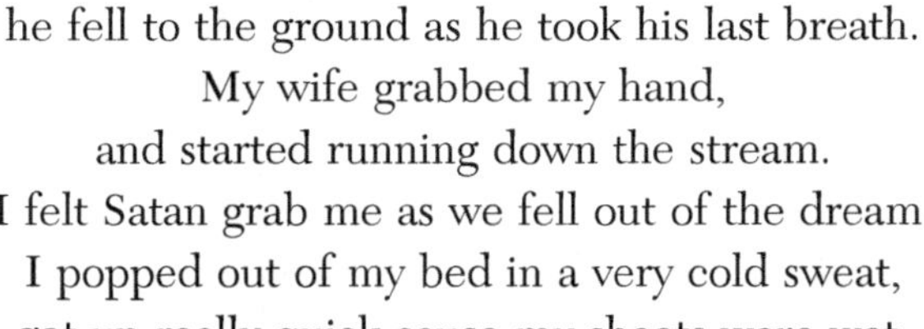

he fell to the ground as he took his last breath.
My wife grabbed my hand,
and started running down the stream.
I felt Satan grab me as we fell out of the dream.
I popped out of my bed in a very cold sweat,
got up really quick cause my sheets were wet.
I still felt that tug on my shoulder,
that tried to keep me in the dream.
A scary nightmare, at least to me it seems.
I was lucky that my wife loved me enough to
grab my hand and run me out of the dream...

Wait a minute... Who was my wife? Why didn't my dad look like
himself?
And was that really Satan grabbing for me at the end?

Kind of scary isn't it?

"But What Was I Supposed To Do?"

I'm a single father who was having a hard time raising
my son by myself.
(But what was I supposed to do?)
No job, hard time finding one, and no help from anybody,
I needed pampers bad!
(But what was I supposed to do?)
I knew a buddy of mine was getting paid the fast way
by selling drugs. I took him up on his offer to sell drugs
part time. (I did it for my kid. I did everything for my kid.)
Then, after only one month, I became a full time dealer of
cocaine and also the big man on the block. I didn't expect
to be this big or even want to be.
(But what was I supposed to do?)
I ended up getting into a fight over money with another
drug dealer. He said he was going to shoot me so I shot
him and killed him first. Now, the police are looking for me.
(But what was I supposed to do?)
The people on the block kept saying the police are everywhere
looking for me and suggest I hide out with my kid somewhere
safe. So, I moved out of my one bedroom as soon as I could,
and stayed on the down low. Six months passed and I
thought about a lot of things I've gotten myself into in a short
period of time.
(But what was I supposed to do?)
Yeah! That should do it! No police should be looking for

me now. What's done is done. I will start living straight,
get a job and support my son the right way.

Two weeks later, I decided to walk to the store with my
son to pick him up some pampers, forgetting all about
the past. As we get ready to walk in the store, out
of the blue someone yells, "HEY"! As I turned around,
POP! POP! Two bullets to my head before I knew it.
As I hit the ground, my eyes closed. As I forced my eyes
open, for the very last time, I seen a tear fall from my son's
eye. I also see the person who shot me... The drug dealer's
younger brother. Then, I blanked out.

Man! Things look so easy, at first.
You never expect nothing like this.
The moral of this story is that if you're ever down on your
luck, there is always a positive way out, just take the time
to find it so you will never have to say...
(But what was I supposed to do?)

SOMEONE FOR ME

Where the cool air flows on
a summer night
Where bad things happen
that just seem right
Where rain makes the sound
hitting the ground like popcorn
To when the sun rises
on a Sunday morn
From when the weather changes
in a blink of an eye
To see the bright stars
way up in the sky
From sand on a beach
to the depths of the sea
Someone is out there
Someone for me.

My vision is clear
but what I can't make out
Is the inner mysterious in me
that I am about
God has the plan
already in His hand
It is just my mind
that I have to expand

So once I do that
I will know and see
That there is someone out there
someone for me

THE ONE

Every time I write a rhyme you pop into my mind
Not just some but all the time
You got to know how much I care
About you and I'll always be there
For you and no other. You are my lover
Not my mother and I will never try
To cover things up, cause I love you so much
You're warm as a pillow and I feel your touch
I go pretty far but I stand my ground
Like ready for the world let me love you down
There's so much to say and so little time
But as long as I'm yours and you are mine
That's what counts both of us together
I doubt there's a couple that could ever be better
When I first met you it was like a process
But all in all now I know I was blessed
With you, the serious one
Who knows when to stop as well as have fun

MEMORIES

Walking in the park, I remember all the memories
Thinking of the future, present, and how it used to be
We were in love, no doubt in my mind
Staying out late to watch the sunshine
We both had jobs and things we bought
Sometimes we got careless but a least we were taught
To love one another and nothing will shatter
Or break us up because it's mind over matter
We felt the same way when we first met
That is something I'll never forget
Let's be friends that's what you said
I thought the same thing like a book that has been read
I couldn't believe it, but I was told
The ones who think the same would be
Together growing old
Hearing that saying makes me a little weary
Come to find out it was only a theory
But now I know you better and way more longer
So as you know my love for you is stronger
So matter where you're at whether far or near
Brent Jones loves you and I'll always be here

LIFE

Life is funny, you know
You are hoping and praying
It turns out the way you
want it to
When in reality, it never does
People are always going to
Judge you know matter what
Color or creed you are
or even family members
They are on your side
only to a certain extent
They have their own things and
problems to worry about
Things for me in life are looking
rather bleak right now
but I know if I keep moving
things will get better... then worse
again, then better again, then worse again...
but that's life
Something you can't get away from
until it's your time to die
I believe only strong people are sent
to earth
because you have to be strong to deal
with life and God knows that

I guess I can question why am I here
but it won't do any good
I mean who listens
besides this piece of paper
I'm writing on and maybe God if
He's not still mad at me
What's the true definition of life?
Does anybody know?
Does it even matter
Life I mean
You're gonna die one day anyway
But until that time we all
are stuck here on Earth
waiting to die
to move on to the next life
Heaven or Hell, we choose
depending what we do in this life
That's why I say life is funny,
because you never know anything about nothing
except the things you actually see with
your eyes that's in front of you
That's where the faith comes in
I feel like crying but I'm not
Just one of those things in life I guess
Writing actually makes me feel better
because I know this is something that
no one can take away (except God of course)
and will continue to do
until I pass away in life.

BE A FRIEND TOWARD GOD

Be a friend toward God because He loves you
In everything that we say and do
The Lord helps us out through all outcomes
No matter what it is you are gonna have some
But in order for Him to work in your life
You have to believe it's not enough to be nice
He loves us more than we can imagine
If anybody could do it you know the Lord can
He loves us so much even from birth
So no matter who you're with learn to put God first
Then everything around you of course would be great
Cause you're serving the Lord and it's not too late
Do right by Him and good will follow
Knowledge is the key don't let your mind be hollow
Jesus died so that we could live
So don't steal from one another instead why don't you give
Give to the poor give to the rich
And you say "Why" it's a natural gift
That you will receive once you get where you're going
It will be a higher place with the love you're showing
So think positive in all you do
Because God is there and He loves you

Don't fill your mind with things that are dirty
The ones who usually do die at 10:30

Keep your mind clear and alert with power
So you can make it around that 11 o'clock hour
I am really glad that God did send
Jesus Christ to be my very best friend
Life is not easy but God is not hard
If you want Him in your life don't disregard
Read the Word to get to know Him better
I know for a fact that He will not let you down
Because He is always around to keep our feet on solid ground
I'm telling the truth so hear me out
Because God almighty is what I'm about
We all make mistakes but it's just coming back
That we have to remember and keep in tact
Because drugs won't help us out *Oh No*
and sex won't help us out *that can't go*
See and believe what you need to receive
while you read with your mind at ease
Then you will know again and again
That Jesus Christ is your very best friend.

If you're deep in sin and you want to get out
Talk to God because that's what He's about
Now I could stand up here and rap all night
about what is wrong and what isn't right
I know for a fact we are all on different levels
Between God earth ourselves and the devil
All I'm saying is know who you are
And be the best and be the best by far
In whatever you do because God loves you
And not just Him but I do too.

The Dream (Part-II)

In the middle of the ocean, what was I doing there?
All I could do was look and stare
Wishing I could get out which I knew I couldn't
So I sat in the boat until the dream was over
Over? What's that? My dream was just about to begin
As I sat there I thought in my mind
What am I gonna go through this time?
I admit I was scared
And I think fear itself knew that
That's when it happened...
Everything started to get dark while deep in a fog covered
the ocean
It got to the point where I couldn't see a thing
Then a voice called out with a quiet roar
Could this be the voice from the dream before?
It said "Take the paddle that's in the boat"
I'll guide you out while you still float
While I still float? What does it mean?
This isn't a nightmare it's just a dream
So I keep telling myself
I picked up the paddle and did what it said
which was start paddling fast or soon you will be _ _ _ _
The voice stopped/just like in the first dream
But I had a feeling... water!
The boat had a hole in it and water was coming in fast

I started paddling while the voice was telling me which way to go
The water in the boat was rising toward my ankles
Then I realized the cold chill that came over me
As the fog started to clear up
I felt out of luck
Was this it?
Up ahead what's that?
A waterfall about 20 feet tall
Then I heard the voice laughing
as I was getting closer to my problem
By this time the boat had sank
I found myself in the cold current of the water
As the waves were pulling me I knew I was through
There is nothing else I could do
So as I got closer I prayed to God as I closed my eyes
I saw nothing but fog
Boy! At last I awoke from the dream
Thank God for that! But is it really over?
What about the voice that was "so called" helping me out?
Who was it? A lot of questions to be answered
but I guess I wouldn't really want to know...
or would I?

A Casualty Of Death

A casualty of death in the streets it's called a war
that nobody wins it's the worse that I ever saw
being getting did if not getting it done facing all
your problems with a knife a handgun
My boy named Ricky everybody called him Rick
grew up around the way in the South East Project's
Drugs for a living was the way to survive
so that's what he did every day to get by
He sold here and there until all the drugs were gone
Didn't care anywhere and thought his life would be
Being locked up was a very bad sign
After that it's just a matter of time
That my boy got popped with five bullets to the chest
Over two bags of cocaine and a half pound of sess
A nigga living large but now a casualty of death
Hit the ground with a sound and to take his last breath
Slain to the game and ashamed to be a name
Now with his family there's pain and nothing else to gain
Just one drug dealer who was doing things his own way
Once in the business someone always has to pay
So stick to a good plan and do what you gotta so
Today it was Rick but tomorrow could be you!

Blood Brothers

Blood is thicker than water
I heard that saying before
Even though that's true
As the sky is blue
To me there's much much more
God made people different colors
For a reason only He knows
But we know that
whatever the fact
His love He always shows
Inside were all blood brothers
No matter what color we are
That's just how it is
cause we all were kids
Fell and got a scar
Once we bleed the blood's the same
Whether black or white
So who's to blame?
GOD? No.
You can forget each other
people blame each other
cause that's what they were taught
So don't love someone
Just for their color
Because inside we're all
Blood Brothers...

Scar For Life

A scar for life is anything but funny
Bad memories about life that was crummy
It happened to the best of us
that usually have a chance
what a mind kicker like
a tune to make a dance
It is done by a family member somebody close to you
and only God knows what you're going through
Unless you have a friend that knows and been there
Then they will understand as the stories you will share
My home girl Lu trice was always being beat
By her father on the street until off her feet
And he didn't care where or who was even watching
When we yell STOP he said he wasn't stopping
He beat her so much that he thought it was okay
To be kicked and beat by her father everyday
When Lu trice was little she was thrown in the tub
And her father used to make her eat the soap suds
Then he would feel on Lu trice I mean every part
Until her pride was gone also her heart
Her mother died when she was eight years old
She was murdered in the sleep but nobody told
Now Lu trice was a love slave for her own father
Everyone knew it but would never be a bother
Until Lu trice's aunt was finally fed up

She called the police because she had enough
The police broke in the house with a warrant to arrest
Lu trice's father pulled a gun and five bullets to the chest
was the outcome of the draw as her father hit the floor
Lu trice was standing there in the room and saw it all
bad memories with a lot of strife
It appears to be clear that's a Scar for Life.

Jesus Is A Friend

The Lord is there
with the Lord you should always feel safe
If it doesn't seem right just have faith
Because He is there each day and every hour
Defeating Satan because God has the power
Because he loves us with all His heart
and with His love He will never part
When I go to bed I have no worries
even though Satan tries to come with many flurries
I block him off like hanging up the phone
and then and there he leaves me alone
so there's no problem as you can see
cause the Lord is with you as well as me
No matter where you are or where you go
Jesus got you covered and that you should know
The Lord knows about you so do the same
Don't beat around the bush while playing little games
But some people don't care they think it's a joke
Unlike the Bible that Matthew, John, and Peter wrote
I love people but only some love back
but that's because of one main fact
they don't know the Lord like they should
I don't know why but I wish they would.

THE DREAM

There I was, fighting the dream,
being stuck there forever that's how it seemed.
What am I going to do? I tried to wake up,
but I fell so far down and was really, really stuck,
but by what? There was something but I couldn't see,
too dark but something was holding me.
I tried to get out then I heard a voice,
saying, "Try to get out if that's your choice."
By this time, I was really scared.
Then I thought, "Is this a dream,
or could it be a nightmare?"
There I was, afraid to move,
knowing it could be my life that I could lose.
I dare not say a word as I felt something moist,
right about then, I again heard the voice
saying, "As I'm holding you, something's holding me.
I don't know either, cause I can't see.
I'm not here to harm you, not here to protect you,
just happened to have the same nightmar---"
The voice stopped... What happened? Keep talking!
I felt the cold moist hand that was holding me DROP!
I started falling further and further down,
It felt like forever!
Finally, I felt something that broke my fall,
something moist.. no wet.. no.. oh God.

I wish I could see what's down here!

I got my wish....
I was sinking in quicksand!
All the other bodies were gone
in already and I was next!
That's when I closed my eyes,
as tight as I could and yelled, "JESUS!"
As I was sinking into the monstrous pit.

WOW! What a dream!
As I woke up to find myself in my soft bed.
I took a deep breath while looking at the pictures
of my family by my bedside.
Then, I felt something at the end of my bed,
like a feather rubbing against my sheets.
I pulled the covers off to find...
A few grains of sand on my feet.
Was it a dream???

Trust In Him Every Day

The Lord loves you and that you should know
no matter where you are living or places you may go
He loves everybody and that is a fact
If know nothing else I know you know that
Serve the Lord cause that's a must
And the rap I'm saying is based on trust
He trusts you so trust in Him
Give Him ten percent when the church you walk into
you'll start loving more and meeting different people
But no matter how they act just treat them equal
Then the light in your life will be brighter than dim
So listen to me and trust in Him.

Read the Bible everyday
and if you do you're on your way
You have to stay strong in God's Word
so people can hear what was never heard
The Lord will work and this I bet it
so trust in Him you won't regret it
The Bible will help you when you're down
so keep the faith with the book around
Start with Kings, Samuel or Psalms,
Matthew, Mark, Luke or even John
Just start reading and you will see
just how easy it can be

You may not get through it cause the Bible is long
but you know you're doing right and not doing wrong
Gifts will come to you and then you'll know
you'll go to heaven and heaven you will go
Step by step and play it safe
It's really not easy but go on faith
Try to love Him as He loves you
it may seem hard but it is true
You say you do but then you don't
You say you will but then you won't
Serve the Lord with your mind and health
He is your teacher your leader
when you can't do it yourself
You have to read and don't just skim
and have all faith while you trust in Him.

The First Encounter

We lock eyes
We meet
We walk to each other
We speak.

The first encounter of love
is the best kind
But the greatest encounter
is going through the process of knowing each other.

You tell me your name
I tell you mine
You give me your number
I give you my time
Spending time together
is like a never ending story
floating in the wind.

So light so right
as love is about to begin
A passion of pleasure
is right around the corner
Just turn around and you'll see
the warm wishes and sweet kisses
you'll indulge from me.

IF YOU HAD 24 HOURS TO LIVE

If you had 24 hours to live what would you do?

I know what I would do

24 hours left: I would go back to Cherry Valley and see who still lives in the neighborhood. Then, I would take two hours to spend with Tim and Eddie saying my goodbyes and hang out for another two hours.

19 hours left: I would catch a plane back to Washington.

17 hours left: I would invite my family from New York, my sister, brother, mom and dad and have a big party for six hours.

11 hours left: I would want to spend an hour taking pictures with my boys and family. Then, spend time with just my sons for two hours, telling them how much I love them and showing them with hugs and kisses.

8 hours left: I would sit down and write out my well wishes. That wouldn't take that long maybe 20 to 30 minutes.

7 hours and 30 minutes left: I would try to explain to my mom and dad how special they are and how important they have been in my life.

7 hours left: I would take 6 hours with Clori, Brannon, Brent Jr., Davon, mom and dad to hug and say my goodbyes.

Then, with one hour left, I would go in my room and make peace
with God, and I'm gone.

So I ask you....

How would you spend your 24 hours?

A Love Thought

Nine months from now I'll be a family man
Get a nice gold ring just to put on her hand
Dress up real nice and take her out to dinner
Because no matter what it takes
This girl I'm gonna win her
Although I already have because she's having my baby
I wanted to get married and she told me maybe
I said "Don't you love me?" and she said "Yes"
But there's a lot of things she has to get off her chest
Confused yet hurt I just walked away
Then thought about her time growing up around the way
A beat and battered child with the form of abuse
Never tried to have a guide that was her excuse
I understand in the hood growing up its hard
Because the verbal abuse left an emotional scar
So I helped her with the problem for about a year
It was a hard 12 months but I helped her persevere
The baby was the best thing in our life
Six months later she was my wonderful wife
There was a time I looked back to say "What does this mean?"
That's about the time I woke up from the dream!

The Business Trip

I went out of town on a business trip
I thought about my wife, so I bought her a gift.
After that, I went drinking with the boys.
Drunk they were getting, getting loud making noise.
I only had a few but that was enough,
because I'm not a big drinker, I was kind of messed up.
Any old way, I left the bar, went across the street to get in my car.
Then, the next thing I know, right out of the blue,
a voice behind me said, "Don't I know you?"
I turned around just to see who it was.
Didn't recognize her face, but she still gave me a hug.
I told her like this, "I don't mean to be rude,
forgive me if I'm blunt, but who are you?"
I'm your wife's friend, Pam. You don't remember me?"
I used to live down the block when I was in D.C.
I still didn't remember but I said, "Hi!"
"It's good to see you again. Now, okay, bye."
I jumped in my car and drove off fast.
I concentrated on my driving so I wouldn't crash.
With these drinks in me, I still had a buzz.
At this point, I wasn't sleep but wish that I was.
So, I got to the hotel still in one peace.
I retired to my room, to get me some sleep.
I got in the bed and begun to snore.
Right about then, I heard a knock at the door.

                                    by Brent Jones

I opened the door, it was the bellboy with a letter.
He gave it to me and asked, "Do you feel better?"
I told him, "No. You have to go. Don't bother me no more."
Then, I slammed the door.
I jumped back in bed to get some zees.
That's when the phone rang, I yelled, "Who could it be?!"
The phone rang, loud, six times in a row.
So, I finally picked it up and said, "Hello?"
"Hi. It's me, Pam, once again.
I followed you to your room, now can I come in?"
I said, "Lady are you crazy? I don't know you from Eve.
If you're at the hotel, get out of here! Leave!"
That's when she started crying, saying she was alone.
Then, she begged and pleaded for me not to hang up the phone.
That's when I cut off my light and said, "Pam, you're out of luck.
I can't do nothing for ya." That's when I hung up.
Finally, it was quiet when I went to lay down.
I wasn't asleep five minutes when I heard a loud sound,
coming from the room right across from mine.
I couldn't lay down. I couldn't unwind.
So, I opened my door and went across the hall.
I got to the room and yelled, "Shut up, y'all!
It's bad enough you're fighting while ya stomping your feet.
But, if you need to throw down, then fight in your sleep!"
Things got quiet. I was happy for that.
So, to my room I started heading back.
Didn't think about a thing until I got to my door.
Then, I realized I was locked out on the fourth floor!
Upset I was. Pissed off. You're right!
I couldn't believe this was happening
all in one night.
So, three flights I walked up, which was no joke.
I would have taken the elevator,

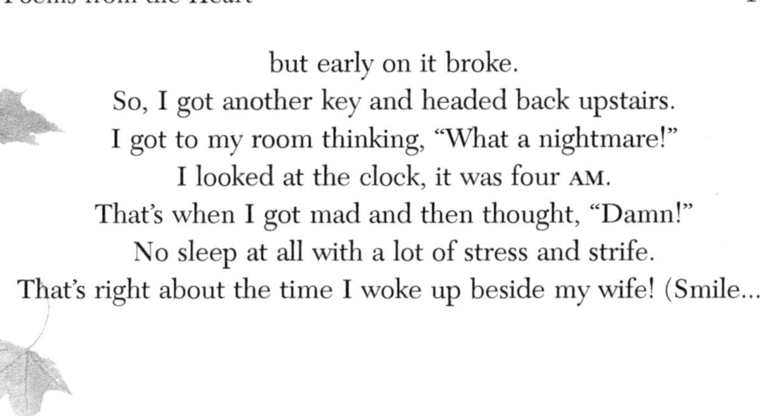

but early on it broke.
So, I got another key and headed back upstairs.
I got to my room thinking, "What a nightmare!"
I looked at the clock, it was four AM.
That's when I got mad and then thought, "Damn!"
No sleep at all with a lot of stress and strife.
That's right about the time I woke up beside my wife! (Smile...)

A PRAYER TO GOD

God, please change my life for the better next time,
to be the best husband I can be,
with the peace of God in my mind.
I don't know my future,
but let me learn from my mistakes,
and give me Your wisdom,
no matter how long it takes.
I want to love You, Lord, and do nothing but Your will.
When my mind starts to wander,
give me the power to be still,
to listen to Your words and follow Your voice,
to hear you with my spirit,
so I always make the right choice.
This chapter is closing in my life,
and I have to let it go.
You've been with me all this way in faith so I know,
it's time to do my part and give You all of me,
so I have a really good chance,
at who you called me to be.
You said obedience is better that sacrifice,
and I disobey a lot,
but now I want to make it right,
only in YOUR sight, with everything I got.
Thank You, Lord, for listening, from poem turn to prayer
and having faith, knowing, that my life is still growing,
with You always being there.

THE ONES THAT GOT AWAY

I was laying on my bed on a regular day,
thinking about the ones that got away.
It was a few years ago, just to be exact,
hanging with my boys, Eddie, Tim and Zack.
We all agreed to get away for the summer.
I remember real well cause that's
when I bought my new Hummer.
We took off to the beach on the Maryland coast,
me, Zack and Eddie had money,
but Tim had the most.
So, we stopped at the store and Tim bought the snacks.
Then, as we were pulling off to go, I happened to look back,
to see this fine girl that brought tears to my eyes.
When she came up to me, I was really surprised.
She said, "Hey. How are you doing? My battery died.
I need help, right now, cause I've already tried,
to turn the car over and it just goes 'click'.
I don't know if it matters but my car is a stick."
I said, "It really doesn't matter if it's a stick or not.
I'll help you, anyway, cause you look hot!"
So, we got to the car, and there were three of her friends.
That's when we said, "Now the fun begins."
So, we all took a lady, and went to the coast.
My lady was the best looking so I started to boast.
I looked her in the eyes and said, "I'm glad you came.

But through all of this drama, I never got your name."
She said, "Just call me the unknown girl from around the way."
I looked her dead in the face and said, "What did you say?"
"I'm just playing, boy. My name is Shay.
My girls names are Kim, Lisa, and Johnnie May."
We got to the beach about a quarter to twelve,
stepped in the sand and began to yell,
cause it felt really good to be out the truck,
and to be with Shay. I felt in luck.
We all settled down in a comfortable bit.
Then, we took out our blankets and began to sit.
We talked for hours. Everything was in order.
That's when Eddie, Tim and Zack took their girl's in the water.
Shay and I decided to take a walk on the beach,
holding hands in the sand made it really complete.
But, while we were walking, we ran into her X.
That's when I thought to myself, "Man dag, what's next?"
He was jealous, of course, cause he wanted her back.
That's when I seen my boys, Eddie, Tim and Zack.
They seen me, too. So, over to me they ran.
We beat the guy up and put his face in the sand.
We punched him in the face, and gave him a couple of lumps,
stepped on his feet and then dared him to jump.
He said he had enough and please leave him alone.
He was so damn scared, he ran all the way home.
When we jumped on her X we really turned it on.
That's when we turned around and the girls were gone.
Tim said, "Where did they go, man? This ain't right."
We looked all day right into the night.
When we got to the truck on the window was a note.
It was from the girls and this is what they wrote:

All four of you are fake, with your kisses and hugs,

but we seen the real you. You all are plain old thugs!
Beating that boy until he couldn't stand up,
that was really messed up, so with US, you're out of luck!
Why don't you go home and play with your toys.
You can be men, because you acted like boys.
So, we came from the beach right up to your truck,
popped the back hood and took all of your stuff!
We thought you were genuine. We thought you were smooth.
We thought you were nice. We thought you were cool.
But now, we see differently with your messed up ways.
So, there's only one more thing that we want to say:
Don't try to be big when you know you're not.
And don't brag about the things that you ain't got,
cause sooner than later in that lane you cruise,
but at the end of that road you will surely lose.
So this is from Shay, Kim, Lisa and Johnnie May,
the ones that were yours, but now the ones that got away!"

THE TRAGEDY

A 17 year old boy named, Steve, is waiting for his mom and dad to leave to go to the movies. As Steve's parents leave, they tell him not to drive the other car while they are gone. He said, "Okay. No problem" with a slight grin. Once they pull out, Steve calls his buddy, Rod. "Hot Rod", the girls call him cause he was known as a pretty boy. Steve said, "I'm on the way to come get you with the car." Rod said, "Cool." So, in the car that Steve's parents told him not to take out, he took off.

Steve picked up Rod and their two girlfriends to joy ride. They rode for an hour. Then, Steve decided to get on the highway. Faster and faster they go – 80, 90 mph… music blasting. The next thing you know, a cop car pulls up behind them, with the siren on full blast. Steve gets scared and tries to out run them. Rod and the girls told Steve to stop. "Too late," Steve said, "I gotta out run them." At this point, Steve was at 100 mph.

Steve, then, started thinking about what his mother and father said about not taking the car. He wished he was back home in bed. As Steve was daydreaming, he didn't hear his friends, Rod and the girls, scream "Watch out!" Steve, then, realized where he was, but it was too late. The car jumped the ramp into the oncoming traffic. At 100 mph, they had a head-on collision with another car and killed the people in the other car, instantly. Steve and his friends also died in the crash. But here's the kicker, the police found out that the people Steve killed… the ones in the other car… were his parents coming back home from the movies. That's messed up, ain't it! The moral of the story is: no matter how it sounds, do what you're told to do because if you don't, you never know who you might *RUN INTO*…

HARD LOVE

Love of sorrow falls
with a lonely cry
as each tear rolls
to the floor from my eye
Why do I cry?
Because once long ago
Love lived in my heart
Also in yours too
but now we are apart
Actually it's a good thing
in some ways
that were not together
because through the
happy times
there were storms
from the days on end
As the new storms
were just about to begin
I thought love made
everything better
Boy, was that a joke
If you're in love looking out
It's really hard to say
But when you're out of love looking in
you understand more
and more every day.

A Friend Like You

A friend like you is someone who cares
A friend like you will always be there
And I know you will because you're that special lady
Who will mostly say "Yes" instead of "No" or "Maybe"
That's a friend.

A friend like you means more than you'll ever know
With a special relationship that will hopefully grow
You are there for me and that's what I see
And now I am here for you and all that you go through
I want to be in your life as long as you let me.

If I take my time I think that is the key
Learn not to say so much to run you away
To keep you I would please you in any way
Does that sound wrong? It sounds kind of funny
But it's true because you've been there for me
in my hard times and I want to be there in yours
to share certain feelings that we both can feel together
Because that's what a real friend like you is all about.

Even though I have a kid you do understand
You stayed in spite of it
When others would have ran
Thank you for being a friend
A friend like you.

"When I'm Alone"

When everything's quiet and nothing's going on, that's when it usually happens. It's like an electric shock wave goes through my body and my mind can't comprehend all the thoughts that hit me, all at one time... when I'm alone.

You can be alright throughout the day because the true thoughts of who you are or how you feel don't betray you when you're busy and have lots to do. Your mind is somewhere else, swimming in the busyness of life. But, once things get quiet and nothing else is going on, all the thoughts you never knew were there hit you like a high powered lightning bolt that you can't control... when I 'm alone.

When I'm alone for a period of time, my thoughts and emotions become one. That's the time when I can't escape my past – things that I wanted, places I wish I was at, and people I was with. All of this thinking can become an emotional roller coaster, sometimes. Especially, if you have any regrets about something or someone. At night is when all of these things hit me... when I 'm alone.

WHEN I KNOW

When I know you love me I will get you a ring
When I know you don't care I will do my own thing
When I know you'll back me up in everything that I do
I will start loving enough to do the same for you.

When I know, in our relationship, there is not a gap
I can start feeling better about giving more back
When I know these things when I see these things
When I feel these things I feel who wouldn't give his life
for a woman that is real?

You need to know that I care for you
But if you really don't know then do what you do
You can go your own way and I will go mine
It will hurt for some time but eventually be fine
But in my heart truly I don't want you to go
And will start giving more back as soon as I know.

WHY AM I HERE?

Why am I here?
Here on this earth December 17th
was a mistake since birth
I don't have a clue of why You did what You did
Put me here since I was a kid
I wish I were dead
Please kill me now
It would be a relief
and I'll show you how
Put me to sleep
into a deep sleep
Then don't wake me up
and my soul You'll keep
if that is Your choice
But if not I'll understand
I've always been a boy and never a man
There are things I asked You that You never told me
Why is that?
How is that?
Is it that I never took the time to see?
O well I'm in hell either way it goes
I'm only kidding myself and everyone knows
that something is wrong
There's something going on
But thank You for my kids

Whatever I did
it must have been right
for them to be born
But I wish I was gone
Gone where?
Somewhere else out there
take me away where I feel no pain
And pain doesn't feel me
where I can breathe
fresh air out there
Can you see it my way Lord?
Just a little is not a lot
or do You care?
If I die by being shot
Where do I go?
Only You know?
I hate being here, but I do love my kids
Is it something that I did?
I hope everyone just leaves me alone
Maybe I'll find myself
Maybe I won't
Why Am I Here???

School Love

It happened one day, all at once, like a Whitney Houston song
My friends just laughed, but I was proving them wrong
The new girl in school, I just had to make her mine
Because something like that was hard to find
The way she walked, she had an elegant style
She didn't talk much, but a beautiful smile
Her clothes were unique, no women can touch
The girls tried to keep up, but the comp was too much
She had a nice shaped body, with looks that could kill
And when I past her in the hallway, my body caught chills
Pretty brown skin, you can adore
And a straight "A" student, who could ask for more
Her rapture perfume it smelled so nice
Made me get out of my seat just to pass her twice
When I got home from school, she was on my mind
And when she entered a room,
it's like a ray of sunshine that hits the wall
and makes the clouds disappear, not lying at all
Just being sincere she's a talented girl
with one smooth voice, to pick her as the winner
is the natural choice
She sounds so good it makes the others sound dead
and whatever she does, she's a step ahead
every time she sings it make my toes keep on tappin
We both fell in love and this is how it happened

I walked up to her
and I said "Hello"
She said, "How ya doing? But I got to go"
Then I said, "Okay. But can we talk later on"
She said "Cool" winked her eye and her word is born
I made the first step to walk over and speak
So I sat back and chilled as later on became a week
I couldn't wait no longer so I approached her again
I told her my name and I was considered a friend
She said her name was Shay
then started walking away
So I left her alone all day that day
Then I never forget it, cause it happened so fast
It was when I sat down in third period class
She walked up to me so fine and slim
And said, "Meet me after school. I'll be in the gym"
So I met her in the gym
And we talked for some time
Then she gave me her number and I gave her mine
We talked every night on the phone was so cool
But even after that I would walk her home after school
A month went by and I was wondering why
I didn't ask her to be my girl
Like I was afraid to try
The hell with this, as I thought to myself
And asked her to be my girl
As we were walking to Health
She said "Yes" as her head she nodded
Love was in the air
And that is how it started.

SEIZE THE MOMENT

I seize the moment, girl, to be with you always
The way you carry yourself got me caught up in a daze
You're not just any angel, you're my angel above
I'm Chili B, as you can see and exploring with love
Mr. Right is in your life and you got to admit
The flames are high so take a sigh as the fire is lit
Press to do my best to be nothing but real
Plus confidential and essential is a part of the deal
I don't but abide you're my heavenly queen
On the throne to call your own with me as your king
I wish to take you out on the beach and to the shore
Walk hand in hand cause it's you that I adore
When I see you coming I dress to impress
Because anything less wouldn't be the very best
The slow jam is kicking and the pace is always steady
With the beat I turn the heat up so we can get ready
To fall in love with a rhyme like this
Not to miss but to kiss as we both
SEIZE THE MOMENT...

To me love is just a word but the feeling you feel
Is the only thing that makes the word love for real
You're my number one lady and here I'll stay
With intellect and no neglect every step of the way
A great relationship from beginning to end

Because you're not just my lover but my very good friend
Who likes to be every night of the week
As I love to be with you and no one else to seek
If you were a queen without a doubt I would bow
If you give me something I couldn't do then I would say how
If you needed your space then I would leave you alone
If you wanted a new house we would get a new home
When we first went out on our incredible date
We had so much fun that we came home late
When I wanted to hold you
you told me to seize
But as the date when on there was a big increase
So as before we should endure a great passionate kiss
Something that I miss as we both
SEIZE THE MOMENT...

What's Important To You?

What's important to you...?
Is it the house you live in or the car you drive
Is it the kids you're raising or the secrets you hide
Is it a promise you kept to someone else but ending up breaking
that promise
when they needed your help. How about your job and the money
you make
or being a good Christian when inside you're fake?

What's important to you…?
Is it running around every chance you get while your mate gets
tired of all your shit
Is it important to spend time with your kids and have fun
Is it important to spend time with your spouse one on one
Is it living life to the fullest without any kind of regret or regret-
ting your past
with the chances you had but blew all the goals you have met?

What's important to you…?
Taking long walks at night in the dark
Believing in something to show you have heart
Fighting in a war so others can have peace
Then going back to war until all the fighting ceases
Is it watching TV or driving a car or getting drunk every day at
the same old bar?

What could be important...?
Is it just peace in your life or on the opposite side could it be
strife
Have your own business working for yourself
Instead of making it working for someone else
Enjoying my kids while they are still young
So when I get old we'll remember all the fun
Taking a cruise on an open sea
A seven day cruise is the place for me
Could it be laying down looking at the sky
While the world's in a hurry passing you by?

Would you like to be a singer on a stage show?
Or a rich millionaire always on the go
A teacher teaching kids about everyday life
Or a man being married to a beautiful wife
Well whatever you choose to be
And whatever you choose to do
Give it no less than your best
If it's important to you.

SILENT CRIES

Silent cries from my face that nobody sees
A fake smile from an invisible child
Who only knows but me
Holding all the hurt that I feel inside
While roaming free from within me
all my silent cries.
The pain is so heavy
with the thoughts that I feel
going through this again
God is this for real?
Nobody can see me nobody can hear me
No one can feel my heart
I'm silent as a picture that hangs on the wall
But cries every day in the dark
When is the hurt going to end this time
I know it will
It just takes time.
So much the same but so far apart
It's hard to let you go when you've captured my heart
I hold my phone wishing you'd call
And when you don't for that day it's like hitting a brick wall.
But then again it's good and I 'm glad that you don't
Makes it easier for me because calling you I just won't
My pride is in the way plus this thing just has to end
Especially since you feel that we can never be friends

All my cries have been outside the norm
So it's time to dry the tears pick up and move on
So in closing I say this...
Always know who you are and do the right thing
Don't be led by your heart
When you been lied to and you also told lies
Be prepared to reap your own silent cries.

BACK IN THE DAY

A level of hip hop thrown to the rap game
Where old school rhymes will never be the same
Back in the 80's it was all about fun
Getting paid was secondary with all the raps that were done
Battling was cool back in the day
To see who was the best with the rhymes we would say
Remember Run DMC with the "King of Rock"
or the slang "That's Fresh" and "Tick Tock You Don't Stop"
And having your own crew break dancing if you're able
And the ones that couldn't break were on the turntables
Then there were guys that did nothing but like it a lot
But even still they would carry a slamming boom box
Those times were great really good and okay
The old school stuff way back in the day

I remember when we rhymed we were lyric rhyme sayers
There were no DVD's, CD's, just record players
They had buttons on the side that are now out of date
Like 33's, 45's even 78's
Back then Luther Vandross was a lady killer
Prince cried purple rain and Michael Jackson was a thriller
Anita Baker made Rapture that will never get old
and Janet Jackson made it happen being in control
Slick Rick and Dougie Fresh made it big with Ladi Dadi
Which was a hit everywhere at each club and house party

Ladi Dadi was number one as we all know and they did it again
when they made The Show
MC's back then were simple and precise
With all their rhymes that's what made it nice
Nice and fresh with the rhymes they used to say
The old school stuff back in the day

There were female MC's that had rhymes that were tight
Like Salt N Pepa and MC Lite
Then Queen Latifah with the rap she ran
And UTFO with Roxanne Roxanne
All these rappers always kept it real
And you would like the music and how it made you feel
The name belt buckles with the gold chains
Fresh bally shoes never ever the same color
Cause you always had others different pairs to wear
Because you used to wear your brothers Kangol caps
With the Lee Jeans, Guess was next with Calvin Klein in between
Block parties after dark and the streets were cool
Everybody knew each other and each other we knew
Those clothes were cool right and okay
The old school stuff way back in the day

**Sadé Jones, Davon and Brent Jr at my
parent's home, Mitchellville, MD. 2004**

The Poem To My Wife

People can come and go
But they disappear from view
Because in my heart and mind
I have eyes for only you
Ever since grade school
My heart has been caught
You were once my girl
A price had been bought
When I look at you now
I see nothing but a queen
The most beautiful girl
That I have ever seen
Now that I have you
I would never cheat
That's hard for you to believe
At the signs of defeat
To me you're not a loser
And you never were
Let doubt leave your mind
So that love can occur
Now that I got you I want it to show
And shout it from the roof tops
So that everyone would know
That my heart is here only for you
Which started way back at
Meadowview.

Derodrick Crowder, Brent Jr, Tracy Jones, Brent Sr, Davon, Dericole Crowder at our wedding, Atlanta, GA. May 31, 2014